Level One: Book 4
Breakthrough to Math

Multiplying Whole Numbers

Materials were developed by the Glassboro State College Adult Education Resource Center in cooperation with New Jersey State Department of Education, Division of School Programs, Bureau of Adult Continuing Education.

Materials do not necessarily reflect NJ State Department of Education Policy and no official endorsement should be inferred.

Edited by Ann K.U. Tussing

Curriculum developers:　　Barbara Banks
　　　　　　　　　　　　　Loretta Pullano

New Readers Press • Box 131 • Syracuse, New York, 13210

Table of Contents

	Page
Pre-test	3
Introduction	5
1. Multiplying numbers	6
2. Multiplying 2-place numbers	12
3. Multiplying 3-place numbers	14
4. Multiplying 4-place numbers	16
5. Carrying when you multiply	19
6. Carrying more than once	23
7. Multiplying by 2-place numbers	27
Post-test	31

Designed by Caris Lester,
Marsha Shur, and Chris Doolittle
Typeset by Chris Doolittle
Cover by Caris Lester

ISBN 0-88336-813-7

Printed in the United States of America

9 8 7 6 5

Pre-test

1. $6 \times 7 = $ _____

   $9 \times 8 = $ _____

   $4 \times 8 = $ _____

2. $\begin{array}{r} 44 \\ \times\ 2 \\ \hline \end{array}$

3. $\begin{array}{r} 53 \\ \times\ 3 \\ \hline \end{array}$

4. $\begin{array}{r} 310 \\ \times\ 5 \\ \hline \end{array}$

5. $\begin{array}{r} 7,212 \\ \times\ \ \ \ 4 \\ \hline \end{array}$

6. $\begin{array}{r} 28 \\ \times\ 2 \\ \hline \end{array}$

7. $\begin{array}{r} 674 \\ \times\ 7 \\ \hline \end{array}$

8. $\begin{array}{r} 42 \\ \times 12 \\ \hline \end{array}$

9. $\begin{array}{r} 965 \\ \times 24 \\ \hline \end{array}$

Answers for pre-test

1. 42

   72

   32

2. 88

3. 159

4. 1,550

5. 28,848

6. 56

7. 4,718

8. 504

9. 23,160

If you missed this question:

Study these pages:

If you missed this question:	Study these pages:
1	pages 6-11
2 or 3	pages 12-13
4	pages 14-15
5	pages 16-18
6	pages 19-22
7	pages 23-26
8 or 9	pages 27-30

These people all need to multiply.
Then they can answer their questions.

1. Multiplying numbers

This woman is planning to save $2 a week for 4 weeks.
How much money will she save?
There are two ways to find the answer.

We can add $2 four times like this:

$$
\begin{array}{r}
\$2 \\
2 \\
2 \\
+\ 2 \\
\hline
\$8 \\
\end{array}
$$

Or we can *multiply*.
Multiplying is a quick way of adding the same number many times.

We show we are multiplying like this:

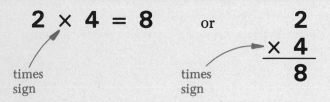

$$2 \times 4 = 8 \qquad \text{or} \qquad \begin{array}{r} 2 \\ \times\ 4 \\ \hline 8 \end{array}$$

times sign

times sign

These are two different number sentences for multiplying.
They say the same thing as these word sentences:

Two times four is eight.
Two times four equals eight.

Multiplying is like adding.
It doesn't matter what order you put the numbers in.
The answer will be the same.

$$2 \times 4 = 8$$
$$4 \times 2 = 8$$

$$\begin{array}{r} 2 \\ \times\ 4 \\ \hline 8 \end{array} \qquad \begin{array}{r} 4 \\ \times\ 2 \\ \hline 8 \end{array}$$

We get the same answer, 8.

Basic multiplication facts

Here are the basic multiplication facts.
You need to know them by heart.
Some people call these facts "the times tables."
Some people learn them in this form:

$0 \times 1 = 0$	$1 \times 1 = 1$	$2 \times 1 = 2$
$0 \times 2 = 0$	$1 \times 2 = 2$	$2 \times 2 = 4$
$0 \times 3 = 0$	$1 \times 3 = 3$	$2 \times 3 = 6$
$0 \times 4 = 0$	$1 \times 4 = 4$	$2 \times 4 = 8$
$0 \times 5 = 0$	$1 \times 5 = 5$	$2 \times 5 = 10$
$0 \times 6 = 0$	$1 \times 6 = 6$	$2 \times 6 = 12$
$0 \times 7 = 0$	$1 \times 7 = 7$	$2 \times 7 = 14$
$0 \times 8 = 0$	$1 \times 8 = 8$	$2 \times 8 = 16$
$0 \times 9 = 0$	$1 \times 9 = 9$	$2 \times 9 = 18$
$0 \times 10 = 0$	$1 \times 10 = 10$	$2 \times 10 = 20$

$3 \times 1 = 3$	$4 \times 1 = 4$	$5 \times 1 = 5$
$3 \times 2 = 6$	$4 \times 2 = 8$	$5 \times 2 = 10$
$3 \times 3 = 9$	$4 \times 3 = 12$	$5 \times 3 = 15$
$3 \times 4 = 12$	$4 \times 4 = 16$	$5 \times 4 = 20$
$3 \times 5 = 15$	$4 \times 5 = 20$	$5 \times 5 = 25$
$3 \times 6 = 18$	$4 \times 6 = 24$	$5 \times 6 = 30$
$3 \times 7 = 21$	$4 \times 7 = 28$	$5 \times 7 = 35$
$3 \times 8 = 24$	$4 \times 8 = 32$	$5 \times 8 = 40$
$3 \times 9 = 27$	$4 \times 9 = 36$	$5 \times 9 = 45$
$3 \times 10 = 30$	$4 \times 10 = 40$	$5 \times 10 = 50$

6 × 1 = 6	7 × 1 = 7	8 × 1 = 8
6 × 2 = 12	7 × 2 = 14	8 × 2 = 16
6 × 3 = 18	7 × 3 = 21	8 × 3 = 24
6 × 4 = 24	7 × 4 = 28	8 × 4 = 32
6 × 5 = 30	7 × 5 = 35	8 × 5 = 40
6 × 6 = 36	7 × 6 = 42	8 × 6 = 48
6 × 7 = 42	7 × 7 = 49	8 × 7 = 56
6 × 8 = 48	7 × 8 = 56	8 × 8 = 64
6 × 9 = 54	7 × 9 = 63	8 × 9 = 72
6 × 10 = 60	7 × 10 = 70	8 × 10 = 80

9 × 1 = 9	10 × 1 = 10
9 × 2 = 18	10 × 2 = 20
9 × 3 = 27	10 × 3 = 30
9 × 4 = 36	10 × 4 = 40
9 × 5 = 45	10 × 5 = 50
9 × 6 = 54	10 × 6 = 60
9 × 7 = 63	10 × 7 = 70
9 × 8 = 72	10 × 8 = 80
9 × 9 = 81	10 × 9 = 90
9 × 10 = 90	10 × 10 = 100

Some people learn the multiplication tables in this form:

Times ✕	1	2	3	4	5	6	7	8	9	10
1	1	2	3	4	5	6	7	8	9	10
2	2	4	6	8	10	12	14	16	18	20
3	3	6	9	12	15	18	21	24	27	30
4	4	8	12	16	20	24	28	32	36	40
5	5	10	15	20	25	30	35	40	45	50
6	6	12	18	24	30	36	42	48	54	60
7	7	14	21	28	35	42	49	56	63	70
8	8	16	24	32	40	48	56	64	72	80
9	9	18	27	36	45	54	63	72	81	90
10	10	20	30	40	50	60	70	80	90	100

(To save space, the 0 facts are not on the table. Zero (0) times anything is always 0.)

Here is how the table works:
Suppose you need to find out how much 5 times 4 is.

Step 1.   Find the first number (5) in the *top* row.
          Put a finger on it.

Step 2.   Find the second number (4) in the *side* row.
          Put a finger on it.

Step 3.   Move the finger on 5 *down* that column.
          Move the finger on 4 *across* that row.

Step 4.   The fingers will meet at 20.
          That is the answer.

So, 5 ✕ 4 = 20

The times tables are very important.
It doesn't matter what form you use to learn them.
You can use the list on pages 8 and 9.
Or you can use the chart on page 10.
But *learn* your times tables!

Exercise 1

Multiply these numbers.

1. $6 \times 4 =$ _____

2. $7 \times 7 =$ _____

3. $1 \times 2 =$ _____

4. $8 \times 9 =$ _____

5. $9 \times 8 =$ _____

6. $6 \times 7 =$ _____

7. $8 \times 6 =$ _____

8. $4 \times 8 =$ _____

9. $10 \times 10 =$ _____

10. $7 \times 5 =$ _____

11. $7 \times 0 =$ _____

12. $3 \times 3 =$ _____

13. $2 \times 10 =$ _____

14. $5 \times 5 =$ _____

15. $5 \times 2 =$ _____

Answers for exercise 1 are on page 12.

2. Multiplying 2-place numbers

Suppose you need to multiply 13 by 2.

13 × 2 = ?
$$\begin{array}{r} \mathbf{13} \\ \mathbf{\times\ 2} \\ \hline \mathbf{?} \end{array}$$

To find the answer, first multiply the ones by 2.

$$\begin{array}{r} 13 \\ \times\ 2 \\ \hline 6 \end{array}$$

Then multiply the tens by 2.

$$\begin{array}{r} 13 \\ \times\ 2 \\ \hline 26 \end{array}$$

So, 13 × 2 = 26

Practice multiplying 2-place numbers

Example 1.   **32 × 4 = ?**

Step 1.   Multiply the ones by 4.

$$\begin{array}{r} 32 \\ \times\ 4 \\ \hline 8 \end{array}$$

Step 2.   Multiply the tens by 4.

$$\begin{array}{r} 32 \\ \times\ 4 \\ \hline 128 \end{array}$$

So, 32 × 4 = 128

Example 2. **41 × 6 = ?**

Step 1.   Multiply the ones by 6.

$$41$$
$$\times\ 6$$
$$6$$

Step 2.   Multiply the tens by 6.

$$41$$
$$\times\ 6$$
$$246$$

So, 41 × 6 = 246

Exercise 2

Multiply these numbers.

1.   31
      × 3

2.   12
      × 4

3.   20
      × 2

4.   22
      × 2

5.   32
      × 3

6.   73
      × 3

7.   62
      × 4

8.   42
      × 3

9.   41
      × 5

Answers for exercise 2 are on page 14.

3. Multiplying 3-place numbers

Suppose you need to multiply 104 by 2.
First, multiply the ones by 2.

$$\begin{array}{r} 104 \\ \times \quad 2 \\ \hline 8 \end{array}$$

Then multiply the tens by 2.

$$\begin{array}{r} 104 \\ \times \quad 2 \\ \hline 08 \end{array}$$

Then multiply the hundreds by 2.

$$\begin{array}{r} 104 \\ \times \quad 2 \\ \hline 208 \end{array}$$

So, $104 \times 2 = 208$

Practice multiplying 3-place numbers

Example 1. $113 \times 3 = ?$

Step 1.   Multiply the ones by 3.

$$\begin{array}{r} 113 \\ \times \quad 3 \\ \hline 9 \end{array}$$

Step 2.   Multiply the tens by 3.

$$\begin{array}{r} 113 \\ \times \quad 3 \\ \hline 39 \end{array}$$

Step 3.   Multiply the hundreds by 3.

$$\begin{array}{r} 113 \\ \times \quad 3 \\ \hline 339 \end{array}$$

So, $113 \times 3 = 339$

Answers for
exercise 2
(page 13)
1. 93
2. 48
3. 40
4. 44
5. 96
6. 219
7. 248
8. 126
9. 205

Example 2.   **532 × 2 = ?**

Step 1.   Multiply the ones by 2.

$$\begin{array}{r} 532 \\ \times \quad 2 \\ \hline 4 \end{array}$$

Step 2.   Multiply the tens by 2.

$$\begin{array}{r} 532 \\ \times \quad 2 \\ \hline 64 \end{array}$$

Step 3.   Multiply the hundreds by 2.

$$\begin{array}{r} 532 \\ \times \quad 2 \\ \hline 1064 \end{array}$$

(Remember to put a comma after the thousands' place.)

So, 532 × 2 = 1,064

Exercise 3

Multiply these numbers.

1.
$$\begin{array}{r} 101 \\ \times \quad 6 \\ \hline \end{array}$$

2.
$$\begin{array}{r} 243 \\ \times \quad 2 \\ \hline \end{array}$$

3.
$$\begin{array}{r} 314 \\ \times \quad 2 \\ \hline \end{array}$$

4.
$$\begin{array}{r} 431 \\ \times \quad 3 \\ \hline \end{array}$$

5.
$$\begin{array}{r} 710 \\ \times \quad 5 \\ \hline \end{array}$$

6.
$$\begin{array}{r} 622 \\ \times \quad 4 \\ \hline \end{array}$$

7.
$$\begin{array}{r} 531 \\ \times \quad 3 \\ \hline \end{array}$$

8.
$$\begin{array}{r} 902 \\ \times \quad 4 \\ \hline \end{array}$$

9.
$$\begin{array}{r} 113 \\ \times \quad 2 \\ \hline \end{array}$$

Answers for exercise 3 are on page 16.

4. Multiplying 4-place numbers

Suppose you need to multiply 1,123 by 2.

$$1{,}123 \times 2 = ?$$

$$\begin{array}{r} 1{,}123 \\ \times \qquad 2 \\ \hline ? \end{array}$$

First, multiply the ones by 2.

$$\begin{array}{r} 1{,}123 \\ \times \qquad 2 \\ \hline 6 \end{array}$$

Then multiply the tens by 2.

$$\begin{array}{r} 1{,}123 \\ \times \qquad 2 \\ \hline 46 \end{array}$$

Then multiply the hundreds by 2.

$$\begin{array}{r} 1{,}123 \\ \times \qquad 2 \\ \hline 246 \end{array}$$

Then multiply the thousands by 2.

$$\begin{array}{r} 1{,}123 \\ \times \qquad 2 \\ \hline 2{,}246 \end{array}$$

So, $1{,}123 \times 2 = 2{,}246$

Answers for exercise 3 (page 15)

1. 606
2. 486
3. 628
4. 1,293
5. 3,550
6. 2,488
7. 1,593
8. 3,608
9. 226

Practice multiplying 4-place numbers

Example 1.   8,122 × 4 = ?

Step 1.   Multiply the ones by 4.

$$\begin{array}{r} 8,122 \\ \times \quad 4 \\ \hline 8 \end{array}$$

Step 2.   Multiply the tens by 4.

$$\begin{array}{r} 8,122 \\ \times \quad 4 \\ \hline 88 \end{array}$$

Step 3.   Multiply the hundreds by 4.

$$\begin{array}{r} 8,122 \\ \times \quad 4 \\ \hline 488 \end{array}$$

Step 4.   Multiply the thousands by 4.

$$\begin{array}{r} 8,122 \\ \times \quad 4 \\ \hline 32,488 \end{array}$$

So, 8,122 × 4 = 32,488

Example 2.   5,213 × 3 = ?

Step 1.   Multiply the ones by 3.

$$\begin{array}{r} 5,213 \\ \times \quad 3 \\ \hline 9 \end{array}$$

Step 2.   Multiply the tens by 3.

$$\begin{array}{r} 5,213 \\ \times \quad 3 \\ \hline 39 \end{array}$$

Step 3 is on the next page.

Step 3.   Multiply the hundreds by 3.

$$
\begin{array}{r}
5\ 2 1 3 \\
\times\qquad 3 \\
\hline
6 3 9
\end{array}
$$

Step 4.   Multiply the thousands by 3.

$$
\begin{array}{r}
5,2 1 3 \\
\times\qquad 3 \\
\hline
1 5,6 3 9
\end{array}
$$

So, $5,213 \times 3 = 15,639$

Exercise 4

Multiply these numbers.

1.	5,142		4.	4,212		7.	3,021	
	× 2			× 4			× 4	
2.	4,010		5.	8,233		8.	7,000	
	× 5			× 3			× 6	
3.	5,022		6.	9,020		9.	7,213	
	× 3			× 3			× 3	

Answers for exercise 4 are on page 20.

5. Carrying when you multiply

Sometimes you get a 2-place number for an answer in the ones' column.
Then you need to *carry*.

Suppose you need to multiply 25 by 3.
First, multiply the ones by 3.

$$\begin{array}{r} 25 \\ \times\ \ 3 \\ \hline \end{array}$$

You get 15.
The number 15 stands for 1 ten and 5 ones.
Put the 5 ones in the ones' column of your answer.
Carry the 1 ten *over* the tens' place of the top number.

$$\begin{array}{r} ^{1}25 \\ \times\ \ 3 \\ \hline 5 \end{array}$$

Now multiply the tens by 3.

$$\begin{array}{r} ^{1}25 \\ \times\ \ 3 \\ \hline 5 \end{array}$$

You get 6.
Add the 1 you carried to this 6.

$$\begin{array}{r} ^{1}25 \\ \times\ \ 3 \\ \hline 75 \end{array}$$

You get 7.
So, $25 \times 3 = 75$

Practice carrying when you multiply

Example 1. **16 × 5 = ?**

Step 1.   Multiply the ones by 5.
You get 30.
Put the 0 in the ones' column of your answer.
Carry the 3 over the tens' place of the top number.

$$\begin{array}{r} 3 \\ 16 \\ \times\ \ 5 \\ \hline 0 \end{array}$$

Step 2.   Multiply the tens by 5.
You get 5.
Add the 3 you carried to this 5.
You get 8.

$$\begin{array}{r} 3 \\ 16 \\ \times\ \ 5 \\ \hline 80 \end{array}$$

So, 16 × 5 = 80

Example 2. **29 × 3 = ?**

Step 1.   Multiply the ones by 3.
You get 27.
Put the 7 in the ones' column of your answer.
Carry the 2 over the tens' place of the top number.

$$\begin{array}{r} 2 \\ 29 \\ \times\ \ 3 \\ \hline 7 \end{array}$$

Step 2.   Multiply the tens by 3.
You get 6.
Add the 2 you carried to this 6.
You get 8.

$$\begin{array}{r} 2 \\ 29 \\ \times\ \ 3 \\ \hline 87 \end{array}$$

So, 29 × 3 = 87

Answers for exercise 4 (page 18)

1. 10,284
2. 20,050
3. 15,066
4. 16,848
5. 24,699
6. 27,060
7. 12,084
8. 42,000
9. 21,639

Exercise 5

Multiply these numbers.

1. $\begin{array}{r} 24 \\ \times\ 3 \\ \hline \end{array}$ 6. $\begin{array}{r} 26 \\ \times\ 3 \\ \hline \end{array}$ 11. $\begin{array}{r} 95 \\ \times\ 2 \\ \hline \end{array}$

2. $\begin{array}{r} 37 \\ \times\ 2 \\ \hline \end{array}$ 7. $\begin{array}{r} 86 \\ \times\ 2 \\ \hline \end{array}$ 12. $\begin{array}{r} 63 \\ \times\ 9 \\ \hline \end{array}$

3. $\begin{array}{r} 17 \\ \times\ 4 \\ \hline \end{array}$ 8. $\begin{array}{r} 64 \\ \times\ 3 \\ \hline \end{array}$ 13. $\begin{array}{r} 53 \\ \times\ 9 \\ \hline \end{array}$

4. $\begin{array}{r} 46 \\ \times\ 2 \\ \hline \end{array}$ 9. $\begin{array}{r} 25 \\ \times\ 5 \\ \hline \end{array}$ 14. $\begin{array}{r} 48 \\ \times\ 5 \\ \hline \end{array}$

5. $\begin{array}{r} 39 \\ \times\ 2 \\ \hline \end{array}$ 10. $\begin{array}{r} 33 \\ \times\ 8 \\ \hline \end{array}$ 15. $\begin{array}{r} 18 \\ \times\ 8 \\ \hline \end{array}$

Answers for exercise 5 are on page 22.

Answers for exercise 5

1.
$$\begin{array}{r} 1 \\ 24 \\ \times\ 3 \\ \hline 72 \end{array}$$

6.
$$\begin{array}{r} 1 \\ 26 \\ \times\ 3 \\ \hline 78 \end{array}$$

11.
$$\begin{array}{r} 1 \\ 95 \\ \times\ 2 \\ \hline 190 \end{array}$$

2.
$$\begin{array}{r} 1 \\ 37 \\ \times\ 2 \\ \hline 74 \end{array}$$

7.
$$\begin{array}{r} 1 \\ 86 \\ \times\ 2 \\ \hline 172 \end{array}$$

12.
$$\begin{array}{r} 2 \\ 63 \\ \times\ 9 \\ \hline 567 \end{array}$$

3.
$$\begin{array}{r} 2 \\ 17 \\ \times\ 4 \\ \hline 68 \end{array}$$

8.
$$\begin{array}{r} 1 \\ 64 \\ \times\ 3 \\ \hline 192 \end{array}$$

13.
$$\begin{array}{r} 2 \\ 53 \\ \times\ 9 \\ \hline 477 \end{array}$$

4.
$$\begin{array}{r} 1 \\ 46 \\ \times\ 2 \\ \hline 92 \end{array}$$

9.
$$\begin{array}{r} 2 \\ 25 \\ \times\ 5 \\ \hline 125 \end{array}$$

14.
$$\begin{array}{r} 4 \\ 48 \\ \times\ 5 \\ \hline 240 \end{array}$$

5.
$$\begin{array}{r} 1 \\ 39 \\ \times\ 2 \\ \hline 78 \end{array}$$

10.
$$\begin{array}{r} 2 \\ 33 \\ \times\ 8 \\ \hline 264 \end{array}$$

15.
$$\begin{array}{r} 6 \\ 18 \\ \times\ 8 \\ \hline 144 \end{array}$$

6. Carrying more than once

Sometimes you need to carry more than once.
Suppose you need to multiply 286 by 2.

$$\begin{array}{r} 286 \\ \times \quad 2 \\ \hline \end{array}$$

First, multiply the ones by 2.
You get 12.
Put the 2 in the ones' column of your answer.
Carry the 1 over the tens' place of the top number.

$$\begin{array}{r} 1 \\ 286 \\ \times \quad 2 \\ \hline 2 \end{array}$$

Then multiply the tens by 2.
You get 16.
Add the 1 you carried to this 16.
You get 17.
Put the 7 in the tens' column of your answer.
Carry the 1 over the hundreds' place of the top number.

$$\begin{array}{r} 1\,1 \\ 286 \\ \times \quad 2 \\ \hline 72 \end{array}$$

Then multiply the hundreds by 2.
You get 4.
Add the 1 you carried to this 4.
You get 5.

$$\begin{array}{r} 1\,1 \\ 286 \\ \times \quad 2 \\ \hline 572 \end{array}$$

So, 286 × 2 = 572

Practice carrying more than once

Example 1.   653 × 7 = ?

Step 1.	Multiply the ones by 7.	
	You get 21.	$\overset{2}{653}$
	Put the 1 in the ones' column of your answer.	× 7
	Carry the 2 over the tens' place.	1

Step 2.	Multiply the tens by 7.	
	You get 35.	
	Add the 2 you carried to this 35.	
	You get 37.	$\overset{3\,2}{653}$
	Put the 7 in the tens' column of your answer.	× 7
	Carry the 3 over the hundreds' place.	71

Step 3.	Multiply the hundreds by 7.	
	You get 42.	
	Add the 3 you carried to this 42.	$\overset{3\,2}{653}$
	You get 45.	× 7
	(Put a comma after the thousands' place.)	4,571

So, 653 × 7 = 4,571

Example 2.   1,874 × 5 = ?

Step 1.	Multiply the ones by 5.	
	You get 20.	$\overset{2}{1{,}874}$
	Put the 0 in the ones' column of your answer.	× 5
	Carry the 2 over the tens' place.	0

Step 2.	Multiply the tens by 5.	
	You get 35.	
	Add the 2 you carried to this 35.	
	You get 37.	$\overset{3\,2}{1{,}874}$
	Put the 7 in the tens' column of your answer.	× 5
	Carry the 3 over the hundreds' place.	70

Step 3.   Multiply the hundreds by 5.
You get 40.
Add the 3 you carried to this 40.
You get 43.
Put the 3 in the hundreds' column of your answer.
Carry the 4 over the thousands' place.

$$\begin{array}{r} 4\;3\,2 \\ 1{,}874 \\ \times \quad\;\; 5 \\ \hline 3\,70 \end{array}$$

Step 4.   Multiply the thousands by 5.
You get 5.
Add the 4 you carried to this 5.
You get 9.

$$\begin{array}{r} 4\;3\,2 \\ 1{,}874 \\ \times \quad\;\; 5 \\ \hline 9{,}370 \end{array}$$

So, 1,874 × 5 = 9,370

Exercise 6

Multiply these numbers.

1. 173
    × 4

2. 287
    × 3

3. 134
    × 6

4. 572
    × 8

5. 438
    × 9

6. 144
    × 7

7. 1,652
    × 5

8. 2,754
    × 6

9. 1,235
    × 8

10. 2,682
    × 7

11. 9,084
    × 5

12. 3,099
    × 6

Answers for exercise 6 are on page 26.

Answers for exercise 6

1.
$$\overset{21}{173} \times 4 = 692$$

5.
$$\overset{37}{438} \times 9 = 3{,}942$$

9.
$$\overset{124}{1{,}235} \times 8 = 9{,}880$$

2.
$$\overset{22}{287} \times 3 = 861$$

6.
$$\overset{32}{144} \times 7 = 1{,}008$$

10.
$$\overset{451}{2{,}682} \times 7 = 18{,}774$$

3.
$$\overset{22}{134} \times 6 = 804$$

7.
$$\overset{321}{1{,}652} \times 5 = 8{,}260$$

11.
$$\overset{42}{9{,}084} \times 5 = 45{,}420$$

4.
$$\overset{51}{572} \times 8 = 4{,}576$$

8.
$$\overset{432}{2{,}754} \times 6 = 16{,}524$$

12.
$$\overset{55}{3{,}099} \times 6 = 18{,}594$$

7. Multiplying by 2-place numbers

Sometimes you need to multiply by 2-place numbers.
Suppose you need to multiply 43 by 12.

First, multiply 43 by the ones' number, 2.
You get 86 as the ones' answer.

```
      43
 ×    12
      86
```

Then put a 0 under the ones' column for a placeholder.

```
      43
 ×    12
      86
       0
```

Now multiply 43 by the tens' number, 1.
You get 43.
Write this 43 next to the placeholder (0).
So you have 430 as the tens' answer.

```
      43
 ×    12
      86
     430
```

Now add the ones' answer (86) to the tens' answer (430).
You get 516.

```
      43
 ×    12
      86
     430
     516
```

So, 43 × 12 = 516

Practice multiplying by 2-place numbers

Example 1.   **45 × 23 = ?**

Step 1.   Multiply 45 by the ones' number, 3.

$$\begin{array}{r} 45 \\ \times\ 23 \\ \hline 135 \end{array}$$

Step 2.   Put a 0 under the ones' column.
Then multiply 45 by the tens' number, 2.

$$\begin{array}{r} 45 \\ \times\ 23 \\ \hline 135 \\ 900 \end{array}$$

Step 3.   Add the ones' answer to the tens' answer.

$$\begin{array}{r} 45 \\ \times\ 23 \\ \hline 135 \\ 900 \\ \hline 1,035 \end{array}$$

So, 45 × 23 = 1,035

Example 2.   **382 × 20 = ?**

Step 1.   Multiply 382 by the ones' number, 0.

$$\begin{array}{r} 382 \\ \times\ 20 \\ \hline 000 \end{array}$$

Step 2.   Put a 0 under the ones' column.
Then multiply 382 by the tens' number, 2.

$$\begin{array}{r} 382 \\ \times\ 20 \\ \hline 000 \\ 7640 \end{array}$$

Step 3.   Add the ones' answer to the tens' answer.

$$\begin{array}{r} 382 \\ \times\ 20 \\ \hline 000 \\ 7640 \\ \hline 7,640 \end{array}$$

So, 382 × 20 = 7,640

Exercise 7

Multiply these numbers.

1. $\begin{array}{r} 36 \\ \times\ 21 \\ \hline \end{array}$

2. $\begin{array}{r} 15 \\ \times\ 12 \\ \hline \end{array}$

3. $\begin{array}{r} 44 \\ \times\ 19 \\ \hline \end{array}$

4. $\begin{array}{r} 23 \\ \times\ 62 \\ \hline \end{array}$

5. $\begin{array}{r} 64 \\ \times\ 40 \\ \hline \end{array}$

6. $\begin{array}{r} 82 \\ \times\ 27 \\ \hline \end{array}$

7. $\begin{array}{r} 275 \\ \times\ 62 \\ \hline \end{array}$

8. $\begin{array}{r} 624 \\ \times\ 39 \\ \hline \end{array}$

9. $\begin{array}{r} 976 \\ \times\ 54 \\ \hline \end{array}$

10. $\begin{array}{r} 307 \\ \times\ 43 \\ \hline \end{array}$

11. $\begin{array}{r} 400 \\ \times\ 72 \\ \hline \end{array}$

12. $\begin{array}{r} 1{,}032 \\ \times\ 21 \\ \hline \end{array}$

Answers for exercise 7 are on page 30.

Answers for exercise 7

1.
```
    36
  × 21
    36
  720
  756
```

5.
```
    64
  × 40
    00
 2 560
 2,560
```

9.
```
   976
  ×  54
  3 904
 48 800
 52,704
```

2.
```
    15
  × 12
    30
  150
  180
```

6.
```
    82
  × 27
   574
 1 640
 2,214
```

10.
```
   307
  ×  43
   921
 12 280
 13,201
```

3.
```
    44
  × 19
  396
  440
  836
```

7.
```
    275
  ×  62
    550
 16 500
 17,050
```

11.
```
    400
  ×  72
    800
 28 000
 28,800
```

4.
```
     23
  ×  62
     46
  1 380
  1,426
```

8.
```
    624
  ×  39
  5 616
 18 720
 24,336
```

12.
```
   1,032
  ×   21
   1 032
  20 640
  21,672
```

Post-test

1. $8 \times 5 =$ _____

   $3 \times 6 =$ _____

   $7 \times 4 =$ _____

2. $\begin{array}{r} 12 \\ \times\ 4 \\ \hline \end{array}$

3. $\begin{array}{r} 31 \\ \times\ 5 \\ \hline \end{array}$

4. $\begin{array}{r} 210 \\ \times\ 6 \\ \hline \end{array}$

5. $\begin{array}{r} 6{,}342 \\ \times\ \ \ \ \ 2 \\ \hline \end{array}$

6. $\begin{array}{r} 47 \\ \times\ 8 \\ \hline \end{array}$

7. $\begin{array}{r} 967 \\ \times\ \ 5 \\ \hline \end{array}$

8. $\begin{array}{r} 34 \\ \times\ 16 \\ \hline \end{array}$

9. $\begin{array}{r} 864 \\ \times\ 46 \\ \hline \end{array}$

Answers for post-test

1. 40

   18

   28

2. 48

3. 155

4. 1,260

5. 12,684

6. 376

7. 4,835

8. 544

9. 39,744

If you missed this question:	Go back to these pages:
1 ──────────▶	pages 6-11
2 or 3 ──────▶	pages 12-13
4 ──────────▶	pages 14-15
5 ──────────▶	pages 16-18
6 ──────────▶	pages 19-22
7 ──────────▶	pages 23-26
8 or 9 ──────▶	pages 27-30